T0349577

DOUGLAS FAIRBANKS: THE MAKING OF A SCREEN CHARACTER

Douglas Fairbanks in THE THREE MUSKETEERS.

DOUGLAS FAIRBANKS

The Making of a

Screen Character

BY ALISTAIR COOKE

MUSEUM OF MODERN ART
FILM LIBRARY SERIES NO.

2

The Museum of Modern Art, New York

© 1940 by The Museum of Modern Art, New York.
All rights reserved.
Facsimile edition © 2002 by The Museum of Modern Art, 11 West 53 Street, New York, New York 10019.
www.moma.org
Library of Congress Control Number 2002108980
ISBN 0-87070-684-5
Electronic typography by Christina Grillo and Gina Rossi
Production by Christina Grillo
Printed and bound by Editoriale Bortolazzi-Stei, s.r.l., Verona
Printed on 135 gsm Gardamat
Distributed in the United States and Canada by
D.A.P. / Distributed Art Publishers, Inc., New York
Printed in Italy

4

CONTENTS

DOUGLAS FAIRBANKS
THE MAKING OF A SCREEN CHARACTER

The process of creating a screen character is now a major element of studio politics. In Douglas Fairbanks' pioneer days it was a matter of luck, talent and hope. To evaluate the Fairbanks screen character against the more subtle and pretentious contemporary process, it is necessary to look at the developed, urban ways of modern Hollywood before trying to decide what made a pioneer in the wildcat days of the 1910's.

I

CREATING A
SCREEN PERSONALITY

We are given to understand that during the past twenty years the business of creating a film star has become a movie industry itself, requiring as it does the health exercise, the voice training, the occasional plastic surgery, the grooming of a merely natural appearance, the timing and schooling of the only career that shows in vivid black on the balance sheet. There is no doubt that it is a very complex process and that the film star is, whatever happens, the object of much sophisticated attention. The routine has been so often rehearsed, it is a wonder any boy or girl worked on by a studio does not automatically become a star. However, most studios will admit a percentage error, and for every star there are usually about a hundred others who defy the magic of the studio grooming. The discrepancy between the producer's hope and the people's adoration may be easy to explain in terms of private lives, mischances, the state of the market. But as a technical problem, it seems to develop somewhere between the make-up factory and the casting director's office. Considered as an important studio executive, the casting director is today the decisive talent in the creation of film stars, for it is up to him to steer subtlety into well-worn grooves or merely to fulfil the preconceptions of melodrama.

Screen acting is not so much the functioning of an individual talent as a presentation of raw human material. Of course, in performance a good deal is left to the actor. But his success depends, more than most publicity writers and fan magazines would care to admit, on somebody's being able and free to make the most of that raw material. Human vanity being what it is, it is extremely unlikely that the actor himself will know what sort of person he ought to play, and most actors are the victims of their looks, not of "the system." Actors tend to give their all and require a flywheel to stabilize their uneven power. This stabilization is, in theory at least, the function of the film director. But the quality of any characterization is due in the first place to the person who did the casting. It is possible to misguide an actor for years by persistent miscasting. Myrna Loy, for example, gave some of the best years of her life to the playing of Oriental sirens who were never conceived, by the writer or director, much above the level of an "inscrutable" as that word is understood in novelettes about life in the Far East. She remained a feature player until somebody cast her as the amiable wife of a playboy-detective in THE THIN MAN Spencer Tracy was cast as a bum, a doughboy, a cryptic Hemingway tough, at a time when nobody would have guessed that he would do best as an affectionate Portuguese fisherman or as Thomas Alva Edison. And Merle Oberon's battle with the adjective "sloe-eyed" was a stalemate until she was, surprisingly, glamorized into naturalness.

There is much more to this than accident. The experience is that of an inoculation that doesn't "take." The point about Myrna Loy is that Oriental glamour was not what she needed in the first place. And Tracy belied his physique. Miscasting is, however, a legitimate and very useful device for comedy if it is consistently and thoughtfully done. For instance, Margaret Dumont, the grande dame who appears in the Marx Brothers pictures, is funny precisely because she seems always to be in the wrong picture. She is not the kind of outraged matron we have been used to in farces. She is, in fact, an outraged matron. This is a ruthless and very successful miscasting and contains some of the pleasures of surrealism. Indeed, from a technical point of view, the whole of comedy hinges on a miscasting of the hero in a normal world; it is droll to think of Buster Keaton as a Confederate general, or Chaplin as a parson, or Bob Hope as an intimate of gangsters. The idea is entertaining because it springs from a wrong view of character.

In any movie not meaning to be a comedy these would be considered as happy comic effects. The casting director would regard them as indulgences of his trade, which is the serious one of creating a world of believable characters. There must be infinite skill in this occupation (in practice there are infinite opportunities for imperception) and it will do no harm to list a few of the ways in which a film character can be made to come alive. It is not that producers consciously work out the type of screen character an actor is to develop. Nor are the following categories of types fixed and separate; they are not prescriptions but analyses. However, as types of screen character they may be more accurate in effect than the casting directory labels[1] are in intention. A sketch of the general situation, with some examples, will perhaps provide a background against which we can more honestly discuss the special case of "Doug," the screen emanation of Douglas Fairbanks.

It seems to be a simpler task to create a female screen character than a male, chiefly because a movie audience demands less variety in female characters than in male. This is not a peculiar preference of movie audiences, it confirms what everybody feels, namely that women in their twenties are primarily objects of desire. A society realistically anxious to reproduce itself will tolerate, at that age, many tiresome individual qualities which later would constitute a positive nuisance. This eminently sensible reason has dictated over the years that in most movies made in the western world the heroine's age is (supposed to be) about 23, the hero between 25 and 30, the villain just over 40. It is considered ungallant to recognize this, but the policies of the studios reflect a strong belief in it; by following up the listing of favorite players in a decade of casting directories it is easy to see that the section "Characters and Comediennes" is, for women, made up not so much of women who are absolutely plain as of women who are relatively old: that is to say, they are women who ten years earlier would have been listed among "Leading Women" and fifteen years earlier among "Ingenues." Studio executives who would doubt the existence of this as a principle would not deny that a film actress can prolong her career indefinitely only if she is prepared in her late thirties to begin playing character parts, as the definition is understood in Hollywood, i.e., mothers, aunts, society matrons, gossips, disappointed spinsters and so on. (Occasionally, a movie is written around an elderly woman considered rather as the "leading woman" than as a "character or comedienne." LADY FOR A DAY was one, but it would count as an experiment. The films of the late Marie Dressler only go to prove the rule, for she is the exception of a popular star whose standing was that of comedienne all her life.) Gladys George and Kay Francis are nearing the crucial stage when they may no longer expect to play romantic roles, which in the movies means playing young unmarried females in their twenties.

Consequently, in looking around for screen material, studio talent scouts are much more interested in surpassingly good-looking young women (or young women who may be made to appear so by the beauty technique of the time)

[1] The Players' Directory of the Academy of Motion Picture Arts and Sciences lists these divisions: Leading Women, Ingenues, Characters and Comediennes; Leading Men, Younger Leading Men, Characters and Comedians; Children, Colored, Oriental.

than in very good-looking young men. The exploitation of this simple and paramount appeal can be more thoroughly shameless, through the agency of the make-up department, as long as cosmetics are taboo to the male in our civilization. So when we start to classify types of female screen character, what we think of is types of beauty than types of talent. Only on second thought do we recall the older talent of Maria Ouspenskaya, Zasu Pitts (once a leading tragic actress and now a comedienne), Elizabeth Risdon, Mary Boland, Marjorie Rambeau. This may sound to some people a shockingly materialistic discussion of an industry that they would prefer to think of vaguely as an art. The movie business is, however, at all times both an industry and an art, and those who can bear to examine their pleasures will find that to analyze motives of studio policy, though it is socially regarded with some cynicism, is in fact a necessary act of criticism.

The most profitable screen heroine that a studio can create—its mechanism will be examined presently—is that of a heroine whose beauty is so overwhelming that it allows her own character never to come into play and therefore never to be called in question. We do not fret over the lack of social purpose, charity, humor or anything else in such perfections of this type as Greta Garbo, Hedy Lamarr, Marlene Dietrich. But nothing is so irritating as the mildly pretty blonde whose beauty is barely acceptable in the first few feet of film and who subsequently has no other charm to offer. Those who fall between these extremes are the majority of stars who combine good looks and certain typical whimsicalities or personal traits of humor, temper, sarcasm— some single quality that is entertaining because it is effective to dramatize. Most moviegoers seem to prefer this compromise-formula as a steady diet, probably because it offers superior beauty to any they are personally familiar with, but is at the same time linked up—by the chosen personality characteristic—with a life they know. Thus Jean Arthur's husky downrightness and loyalty, Claudette Colbert's tongue in the cheek, Carole Lombard's air of honest-to-goodness exasperation, Ginger Rogers' natu-

ral acceptance of hard facts; these are the individual characteristics of current favorites who were all originally consigned to a screen career of solemn prettiness.

The fact that so many stars are originally misjudged in this way does, however, stress the primary attribute of good looks which it is essential for women stars to have, however flippantly it can be disregarded in the later emergence of a distinctive screen character. It also reveals how eager the studios are to see in every girl they choose to groom the type they now know to be ideal—the overwhelming beauty. Very often a star is elevated from the general run of stars and the hope persists for years that she is meant to play nothing less than Cleopatra or Mata Hari. This threatened at one time to ruin the screen careers of Joan Crawford and Katharine Hepburn. This warning signal, both for actress and public, is a disposition to drop her first name and substitute the definite article, La. Here the imposition of what is roughly known as "glamour" was false, since the human characteristics of the victims were too strong to be ignored.

Perhaps the best example of this envied ideal is the screen character of Marlene Dietrich. It may be that Miss Dietrich was not originally surpassingly beautiful or even a good actress. The producer Joseph von Sternberg spotted in her something which could be accented to make her the archetype of an extremely trite romantic convention, namely the lovely siren, the *femme fatale*. To represent this most envied of female characters on the screen is a matter not of subtlety but of degree. The first thing is physically to glamorize the raw material. In her early Hollywood handling, Miss Dietrich was made to lose the air she had of a plumpish German *fräulein*. For the mystery of the *femme fatale* is at this date very well aired. She must lose obvious characteristics of place and age; she must never seem quite real enough for any audience. It is because she has no roots of race or home that she can appear suddenly in strange places, with the unsuspected inevitability of a hurricane; it is because she is this sort of international essence of sin that she exotically blinds the senses of the conventional man with a job to do in a definite place; it is because she has no home, no passport, no humdrum loyalties that the memory can hold her only in permanent soft focus, which is the regular way of presenting her screen image. It is not a hard character to create but the potential material is hard to find, since it seems to require quizzical eyes in a face of broad and handsome bone structure able to take each succeeding layer of eyelash and lip-rouge and grow more bold without growing more ridiculous.

With male stars there are no such opportunities—except possibly in Western films—for simple and lush amplifications of the fantasy life. The male is severely restricted in make-up, though many leading men wear applied hair. Somehow, a dream beauty is not so much in demand among women. Indeed there have been male stars whose natural good looks have had to be toughened and made irregular in order to satisfy the conventional desire for a worthy mate. This restriction—which again is not imposed by the movies but by the tastes of our society—reduces the straight handsome leading man to an insignificant romantic symbol compared with his counterpart in the male consciousness. The most successful male screen characters are accordingly built out of subtler formulae than the females, and their patterns appear to be truer to the actual weave of character in real life. There can hardly be any question that there is a greater variety of character among screen heroes than among screen heroines. The formulae for creating them are numerous; one or two, although highly successful, nevertheless offer a contrast in detail and subtlety, with the direct and powerful screen character of Douglas Fairbanks.

Some obvious ones are: original bad man turned into hero, as with William Powell and Wallace Beery, not by any fundamental change in their personality but by suggesting to the audience a new view of it, and of odd characteristics that were once thought fixed attributes of evil. After a run of villain roles, Powell's parts were written to ingratiate rather than menace, so that his owlish look suggested not crime but the playful tolerance of a man of the world. Similarly, Wallace Beery was doomed to be a villain at a time when the movies were tied to the conventions of the theatre. Florid men with slant eyes were bad men from birth, until it was seen that by making his screen character that of an ugly duckling wanting to help, Beery could be transformed from bad man into lovable cuss.

The most popular formula just now for young heroes, as well as for most unsympathetic parts, is to dramatize a single streak of character. This process applied to female stars is conceived as a sort of human relief to physical beauty and is therefore usually a comic streak. In men it is more commonly a pathetic weakness puncturing the romantic legend of male infallibility and therefore stimulating sympathy. Clark Gable has for long been shown as a quarrelsome male whose devotion to the bottle called for our tolerant aid. Fred MacMurray's tendency to fly off the handle out of self-pity has also cleverly appealed for a large measure of feminine protectiveness. An important variation of this method—it may be quite separate—is the dramatization by accident or design of a streak of character which belongs not to the script but actually to the private life of the actor. The strong and specific appeal of Rudolph Valentino and Lou Tellegen was certainly connected with some undisguised quality in their own rather disappointed lives. The fluency and rightness that James Cagney and George Raft bring to a certain type of small-time hero is made easy for them by their background familiarity with the type and the milieu. Cagney has succeeded as nobody before or since in sharpening a type of American virtue which is excitingly revealed by its elaborate and cocky pretensions to the opposite. It is a bullying determination not to see anybody bullied; it can be met with in life in some cops, foremen, sailors and newspapermen. The actor's technical mastery is obviously invisible to many who think of Cagney as "a rather unpleasant type."

Gary Cooper and James Stewart would appear to be examples of the *romanticizing* of a pervading trait of character, usually whimsicality. This is very close to the Cagney formula, except there is no proof that Cooper and Stewart are like their screen selves in private life. It would be tempting to say that Gary Cooper is so rounded and firm a character that he must be a similar person in private, but it may be no more than longer experience and bitter technical control which makes him today a better performer than James Stewart of what is essentially the same screen character. Whatever is the secret of the method, Cooper is a very successful result, for even his silences—which in life may mean curiosity, boredom, having nothing to say—seem on the screen to be the essence of male self-sufficiency.

Douglas Fairbanks was about as successful as Cooper in giving the impression that his screen self was the whole of him. But the character of "Doug" is still unique in movie history and though its impact on a delighted world audience was direct and real, his screen character was in many ways a fantasy in which a suddenly jolted world could escape its bewilderment. He managed to mate actor and audience to produce a type of pleasure which is closer to old-time vaudeville or that of a jam-session than to an audience contemplating a painting or a play.

It is hard and always dangerous to try to pin down the theatre personality of a famous actor when once the colors have faded. It is complicated here by the confused social attitudes that people took toward the movies during the 1910's and twenties, and beyond. Only small children and the illiterate seemed to enjoy a direct response, one of delighted absorption in the movies themselves. All others hastened to learn a series of shamed social poses (none the less poses for being often perfectly sincere) which moralists, stage people, *littérateurs* and others manufactured for them. It is, of course, the old reflex of "maintaining one's standards" in the face of an apparent threat, a habit which kept the Renaissance so long out of England, Mark Twain off the shelves of Boston and Philadelphia, and which regards a Chippendale chair not as a challenge but as a final model for living. To have had the good fortune to be a small and absorbed child during this period, who learned too late that the movies were a depressed cultural product, makes it possible genuinely to pretend to think Douglas Fair-

banks as important as he seemed to be between 1917 and 1922 and to attempt to look for the elements of his screen character. By the casting directory definition, we shall follow the progress of Douglas Fairbanks from a "Young Leading Man" to a "Leading Man," ending in a final picture in which—to preserve intact his former glory—he deliberately became a "Character or Comedian." More accurately we are looking into the private character of Douglas Fairbanks to see how it was romanticized or recreated to make him become one of the most admired actors of his time and be billed and accepted as "the best liked figure on the screen."

The most sensible approach would appear to be to examine the raw material of his own life and character, up to the time he arrived in Hollywood.

II

THE RAW MATERIAL: DOUGLAS ELTON ULMAN (1883-1915)

Douglas, the son of H. Charles Ulman, a New York lawyer, was born in Denver, Colorado, on May 23, 1883. The family had not been long in the West; the father had gone to Denver to look after some mining interests. Soon after the birth of Douglas, Mrs. Ulman divorced her husband and resumed the name of her first husband, Fairbanks, which her son subsequently used and, in 1900, legalized. There is nothing notably peculiar about the Fairbanks childhood except bouncing good health and a determination, probably sharpened by the divorce, to show exemplary devotion to his mother (he seems to have enjoyed making difficult pledges at an early age and keeping them; one of these was a promise he gave his mother never to touch alcohol, which he never did). He went in turn to the Jarvis Military Academy, the East Denver High School and the Colorado School of Mines.

It is part of the fan magazine tradition that at least one of the parents of a film star who had never expected to be anything but a lum-

berman, garage mechanic or newspaper car-
toonist should be imbued with a deep and daily
devotion to Shakespeare, his enthusiasm in
time seeping irresistibly through to the little
fellow, who feels thereupon commanded to go
to Hollywood and qualify for the lead in THE
GOLDEN VANITIES OF 1941. This tradition has
been printed about the Fairbanks family and
seems to be difficult to disprove. What, however, is undeniably true is that Fairbanks
memorized Shakespeare soliloquies and was
surely taught to say them in the hectoring
Shakespearean tradition of his father's day.
There is a streak of rodomontade in the Fairbanks character which probably responded
with enthusiasm, not necessarily to the Shakespeare text but to the declamatory zest and the
large gestures which were the stock-in-trade of
Shakespearean acting in those days and which
have persisted, especially in the United States,
to our time.

He left high school in 1900, when his family
moved back East, and he was sufficiently in
earnest about the theatre to look around for a
job in it. He managed an introduction to
Frederick C. Warde and was given his first
part, as a lackey in one of Warde's road com-
panies then playing *The Duke's Jester* at Richmond, Virginia. This he apparently regarded as
an experiment, for an untraceable provocation
soon led him to enter Harvard for what is
mysteriously described as "a special course."
At the end of five months, however, the special
course and Harvard College had no further
interest for him and presumably to everybody's
satisfaction he left Cambridge. He did some
Shakespearean repertory under Warde. In 1901,
he made his first Broadway appearance, in support of Effie Shannon and Herbert Kelcey, in a
play called *Her Lord and Master*. This should
normally mark the first stage of a continuous
acting career, but it is typical of Fairbanks that
having achieved a profession (declaiming in
Denver he would probably have reeled at the
notion that he would ever play on Broadway)
he was then ready to take on another. There
was in his mind a definite and romantic pattern
of the things a successful man might be. He was
already an actor. He would now like to be a king

Fairbanks at the age of 21

of finance. He quit the stage and got a job as
an order clerk in the New York firm of De
Coppet and Doremus. He found himself if not
in a key position, at least in a well-oiled one
where a knowledge of the Wall Street jargon
made the wheels go around. This knowledge
everybody seemed to take for granted in him,
a form of confidence that scared him more than
it impressed him. After a few nerve-wracking
errands on which he was entrusted with vital
orders that he had to memorize, as it seemed to
him, in Sanskrit, he left "the Street" forever
before a higher-up should discover his innocence

11

With Hal De Forrest and Thomas A. Wise in the play, *A Gentleman from Mississippi*, 1909

after some titanic deal had foundered. Under perhaps the most sober and least romantic stimulus of his life, he took a job with a hardware firm, for the oldest reason—that he was hard up and needed money for, among other things, the boxing, wrestling and gymnastic lessons he was taking in various gymnasiums around New York. Here he fell in with a couple of football players, and his adventure in hardware became a part of history. He cooked up a scheme to bum around Europe with them. This he did, starting on a cattle-boat and landing at Liverpool with a pay-check amounting to eight shillings. Doing the pick-up jobs of amateur hobos, the trio wandered through England, Belgium and France and came back on another cattle-boat.

In the meantime young Fairbanks had heard about the law and decided it was time to be a lawyer. He took a very brief header into a law course and came up smiling but converted. It was not possible to be a brilliant prosecutor by Christmas and he turned unabashed to roam the other fields in which men had made a dramatic mark. Fairbanks may have been restless, but there is a healthy sign evident in most of his switches of profession: he did not suffer from a literary imagination nor dream merely of being a "great writer, actor, scientist." He was, aside from his own temperamental impulses, genuinely interested in the phenomenon of success and his heroes are a catholic lot. He had an eager respect for a first-rate stockbroker, politician, traveler, lawyer; for most top-flight athletes, aviators and inventors. Thus he turned to the manufacture of machine tools and worked awhile in a manufacturing plant. But of all his professions he still knew most about acting, to which he finally returned in 1902. He joined the company of *The Rose of Plymouth Town* starring Minnie Dupree. A solid piece of luck befell him when William A.

12

Brady, the Broadway producer, took to him and gave him a five-year contract, later extended to seven years.

Throughout this period he played on the road and on Broadway. He did a short stretch in vaudeville, but most of the time he was in New York beginning to make a modest reputation as a breezy juvenile. He married and had a son. Between 1910 and 1915 he was an established Broadway success, never exciting great critical acclaim but sure of his public and himself. He was starred in *Officer 666; Hawthorne, U.S.A.; Frenzied Finance; All For a Girl; A Gentleman from Mississippi; The Cub; A Gentleman of Leisure; He Comes up Smiling; Henrietta;* and lastly *The Show Shop.*

There is by now a solid legend among magazine writers and movie interviewers that Fairbanks was an atrocious stage actor whose Hollywood career was a happy miracle. It is a tale based chiefly on a cruel notice in a Duluth newspaper, on Frederick Warde's account of the Fairbanks Shakespearean style as "a catch-as-catch-can bout with the immortal bard," and on Minnie Dupree's opinion of him as a bad case of St. Vitus' Dance. These opinions are important not as denunciations of an actor but as descriptions of a person. For Fairbanks' stage record remains a creditable one, according to the reviews of his plays that can be dug up and dusted off. It is true that he was high-strung and grinned a great deal. Yet William Brady was a shrewd and prosperous theatrical producer, and unlikely to sign a grin for a five-year contract. It is most probable that over fifteen years Fairbanks learned as much about comedy playing as any other light comedian of the day. It is true that, as it happened, his theatrical record had very little to do with his startling Hollywood fame and with the creation of the screen character "Doug." But he was signed to his first motion picture contract on the strength of that record. The Triangle Corporation at any rate thought him worth $2,000 a week. They regarded him, as in cold fact he was, a Broadway star and a very able light comedian. There was something else which Harry Aitken, Triangle's manager, saw in Fairbanks and which suggested to at least one man

not a different but a more vivid personal success in the new intimacy of the movies. Aitken later recalled this hunch and had the honesty not to claim any foresight of the special Fairbanks gifts; "we picked Douglas Fairbanks as a likely film star," he reported years later, "not on account of his stunts, as the majority think, but because of the splendid humanness that fairly oozed out of him."

This was the raw material which within five years was to be made over into "Doug," so that it was no longer possible to say where "Doug" began and Fairbanks ended: a vigorous, healthy young actor, thirty-one years of age, of an alarming good nature; known to the theatre public as a spirited light comedian, known to his friends as a practical joker, a restless idealist who talked exuberantly in an effort to be vivid; an amateur gymnast and boxer whose hand-stands on chairs and day-time riding, boxing and wrestling were a friendly back-stage joke. This was the Douglas Fairbanks who entrained for Hollywood in the spring of 1915 and who had no plans and little hope for the movies or his future in them. The Triangle offer was almost distasteful to him, as to many another stage actor holding fast to the sentimental pride of the theatre. Frank Case, the hotel keeper and a close friend, pointed out to him that $104,000 a year was a very handsome salary. "I know," replied Fairbanks in a final flutter of dignity, "but the movies!"

III

THE MAKING OF "DOUG"

The idea of signing stage stars to make motion pictures was, in 1915, a dangerous novelty both to stage actors and movie producers, who respectively were haunted by loss of professional dignity and loss of hard cash. When Harry Aitken made the proposal to his employers, the Mutual Corporation, they were unwilling to take the risk. He therefore had to look elsewhere for the backing. He found it in the Triangle Corporation (so called in honor of the producers D. W. Griffith, Thomas Ince and

Mack Sennett), scanned the Broadway season of 1914-15 and contracted over sixty legitimate actors, among them Sir Herbert Beerbohm Tree, Mary Anderson, Weber and Fields, DeWolf Hopper, Billie Burke, Texas Guinan, Frank Keenan, Elliott Dexter, Willard Mack—these were considered the best bets. Also signed were two lesser stars: Douglas Fairbanks, and William S. Hart, who had made a picture or two for Ince.

When he arrived in Hollywood, Fairbanks reported to Griffith, who was to supervise THE LAMB, though Christy Cabanne was scheduled to direct it. After routine tests, during which Fairbanks buoyantly vaulted tables and discommoded the crew—who were suspicious of stage stars anyway—the shooting began. Griffith was engrossed at this period with the power of the motion picture camera to delay the tempo of conventional acting and to focus casual facial expressions into much meaningful detail. Fairbanks bounced rudely into this preoccupation. He tended rather to discard acting than to elaborate it. And Griffith must have reflected a little ruefully that he had taken as much pains with this Aitken find as he was soon to lavish on Sir Herbert Beerbohm Tree and Constance Collier in MACBETH.

There was a further reason why Fairbanks failed to get off to the flying start that Harry Aitken had imagined. The crew that worked with Griffith was a busy unit, jealous of its habits and, as small contented staffs are apt to be, unwilling to change its routine. They took a dislike to Fairbanks not as a person but as a symbol. There had been much speculation over the move to recruit theatre stars, and by the time Fairbanks arrived the crew had come to the conclusion that they were against it. Fairbanks' hearty good nature defeated their expectations but they were not so easily to be denied a little resentment. According to G. W. Bitzer, Griffith's veteran cameraman, they plotted a mild act of malice, seeing to it that Fairbanks was given a wrong and rather ghastly make-up. It is very apparent in the early sequences, especially in the scene on the beach at the end of reel one, when Fairbanks achieves —for the first and last time—a look of ashen

gravity that is hard to credit in a light comedian. The combined effect of acrobatic levity in comedy scenes with strenuous hamming was enough to convince Griffith that there was little hope for Fairbanks in Triangle's ambitious program. He urged him to go into Keystone comedies, where he could skip and jump to his heart's content. Fairbanks was now in Griffith's opinion something of a liability and he was shunted, along with most of Griffith's unsolved problems, to the care of Frank Woods, who acted as a sort of cowcatcher to Griffith productions, sweeping accumulated embarrassments away from the path of the Master.

It is Harry Aitken and Frank Woods who may claim more than anybody else to have made possible the screen fate and fame of Douglas Fairbanks. For one of them sensed, without being able to define, a personal quality in him; and the other knew who could provide and heighten the definition. Frank Woods, too, was probably more interested in people than in actors. He liked Fairbanks and shrewdly guessed that he would probably have much in common with two others on the Triangle payroll—a director and a script writer—John Emerson and the precocious girl scenarist still in her teens, Anita Loos. After a little acquaintance with Fairbanks these two saw that whatever his Broadway reputation had been, the charm of Fairbanks was the bounding trajectory of his private life. By applying their talent to the original Douglas Ulman, somehow there emerged a character whose performance needed the range and movement of the screen and one which a proscenium arch could not hope to frame and perhaps had never held.

Fairbanks so far had failed to make the impression Aitken had hoped; nevertheless, he was very lucky to be entering the movies at this adventurous but haphazard period. For within as short a time as ten years he would have automatically been submitted to the clinical tests and thorough speculations of the studio casting office. He would have been "typed" for several contracts to come and it is doubtful if "Doug" would have emerged by chance or design for a good many years. As it was, he was merely considered an unfamiliar misfit, but after a few films he was given his own writers, a luxury that is nowadays enjoyed only by national comedians whose chief problem is to keep their incomes stabilized at a current frightening peak.

After THE LAMB was finished, Fairbanks went back to New York. Triangle did not think of THE LAMB as a remarkable picture in itself but it happened to be shown on the first Triangle program presented on September 23, 1915,[2] at regular theatre prices, to see if the movies could compete with the theatre's large and respectable middle-class following. It was presented to an audience very different from the nickelodeon addicts for whom the movies had hitherto been considered fit entertainment. Jan Ignace Paderewski was a guest of honor, and celebrities like Howard Chandler Christy, Irvin Cobb and Rupert Hughes were on hand to show there was no ill feeling towards the motion picture's new pretensions. The next morning the *New York Herald* declared, "The three-dollar movie is a reality!" The movies were, socially at least, no longer vulgar. The Triangle chiefs could breathe a grateful sigh and continue their policy of regarding stage and movie actors as henceforth a common caste.

Of THE LAMB itself, the reporters praised its pace and thought Fairbanks a lively hero. Griffith's disappointment must have been softened when he read that "the dash of the mounted troops to his aid was reminiscent of the Ku-Klux-Klan raid in THE BIRTH OF A NATION."

Fairbanks went back to Hollywood and invited his friend Frank Case to go along with him. Case has given a good picture of this trip[3]:

> "We occupied a compartment on the train and there were the usual number of tricks played, in most of which I was on the receiving end. At La Junta, Colorado, I was awakened very early one morning to find a big Indian, face painted, blanket, feathers

Charles Chaplin, Mary Pickford, Douglas Fairbanks shortly after the incorporation of United Artists, 1919

> and all, sitting on my berth bending over me . . . I did succeed in putting one over on Doug, though. It was his habit to remain pretty much all day in the compartment in pajamas and bathrobe, sending the porter out at every stop for fruit, candy, papers, ice-cream, or whatever was offered for sale at the different stations . . ."

Case told the porter that "Fairbanks was a mental case on a strict diet" and that "the patient's orders had better be politely ignored."

For a day Fairbanks could get nothing he asked for.

Fairbanks all his life loved this rather elaborate sort of joshing and would often hold up the making of a picture, at considerable expense, to change into costume as alien as possible to the period and style of the picture. The Hollywood they saw was then, in Case's words:

> "a quaint and lovely place. We used to ride horses all over the country from Beverly Hills in any direction, cross-country down to the Wilshire district or in the other direction up through the hills. Sometimes

[2] The other features: Ince's THE IRON STRAIN with Dustin Farnum, and Mack Sennett's MY VALET with Raymond Hitchcock and Mabel Normand.
[3] *Tales of a Wayward Inn*. New York, Frederick A. Stokes Company, 1938.

there was a dusty road, sometimes no road."

In this milieu Fairbanks could call his private life his own more than he had been able to in New York. The staff of the Triangle studio soon learned that his cavortings during the shooting of THE LAMB had been no show-off antics but the involuntary expression of his disposition. Fortunately, the directors who handled his pictures had the vision to incorporate them into his work. And chief tribute is due Anita Loos and John Emerson, who probably saved Fairbanks from temporary extinction or at least from migrating to another studio. They were Fairbanks' favorite writer-director team and he took them under his wing when he formed his own producing company at the end of 1916. They cannot be credited with inventing the Fairbanks screen character, but they were the first to indicate what it might be and how much the restless personality of Douglas Fairbanks should color it.

During the busy year of 1916, Fairbanks was in eleven pictures—more than a quarter his entire output—and Loos and Emerson were involved singly or together in only four of them. Allan Dwan is also a name worth mentioning, for by and large he was the best of the Fairbanks directors and had the longest successful

association with Fairbanks. Of the twenty-six Fairbanks films done before the incorporation of the Big Four (Griffith, Fairbanks, Chaplin and Pickford) into the United Artists in 1919, Loos and Emerson were in charge of at least seven, Allan Dwan of six, Joseph Henabery and Christy Cabanne of two each. Fairbanks himself directed one (ARIZONA), which is probably his worst film. It was evidently better for somebody else to watch the movie in motion. What was needed was no rare skill, but a willingness to let Fairbanks' own restlessness set the pace of the shooting and his gymnastics be the true improvisations on a simple scenario. Out of this amiable understanding, which Fairbanks achieved with most of the people he worked with, the character of "Doug" rapidly evolved.

Most of the 1916 stories were conventional comedy—melodramas decorated by acrobatics. In HIS PICTURE IN THE PAPERS, the movie audience was offered a six-round bout between Fairbanks and a professional fighter, a high dive from an Atlantic liner and a leap from a train. In THE HALF BREED he fought a forest fire, in THE GOOD BAD MAN demonstrated his climbing prowess in a Western canyon, in THE MYSTERY OF THE LEAPING FISH he was proclaimed to be "a human submarine." But the movie public looked beyond this obvious melodrama and was intrigued by other aspects of the Fairbanks hero.

At a difficult time in American history, when the United States was keeping a precarious neutrality in the European war, Douglas Fairbanks appeared to know all the answers and knew them without pretending to be anything more than "an all-around chap, just a regular American" (THE AMERICANO). The attraction of this flattering transfer of identity to the audience did not have to be obvious to be enjoyed. The movie fan's pleasure in Fairbanks might have been expressed in the simple sentence of a later French critic: "Douglas Fairbanks is a tonic. He laughs and you feel relieved."[4] In this period of his earliest films it was no accident that his best-liked films should

THE GOOD BAD MAN, with Bessie Love, 1916

[4] Gheri, Alfred, "Reflexions sur l'art de Douglas Fairbanks," *Ciné-a-Ciné*, Paris, Nov. 1, 1927.

have been HIS PICTURE IN THE PAPERS, REGGIE MIXES IN, MANHATTAN MADNESS, and AMERICAN ARISTOCRACY. These were respectively about the American mania for publicity; about a society playboy who was not above finding his girl in a downtown cabaret and fighting a gangster or two to keep her; about a Westerner appalled at the effete manners of the East, and about a Southerner of good family who married into "bean-can" nobility, and was healthily oblivious of any implied snobbery. Here already was the kernel of a public hero close enough, in manner and get-up, to contemporary America to leave his admirers with the feeling that they were manfully facing the times rather than escaping from them. It is important to insist on this transference of flattery from the screen to the audience, for it is a necessary step in the process of becoming a public hero in almost any field. The Fairbanks screen character was forming at a time when the American and European peoples were badly in need of just such a rousing popular reassurance.

The 1916 movies did not release this hero full-blown but sketched his cartoon: a young vigorous man as uncompromising as his splendid physique, unfazed by tricky problems of taste and class behavior, gallant to women, with an affection for the American scene tempered by a wink. It had already two of the elements of the finished portrait which may be roughly described as popular philosophy and athletics. Fairbanks' decision to form his own company at the end of 1916 filled in the third element—the necessary background of showmanship.

These three elements are visible at different times of his career; his popular philosophy appears mostly between 1917 and 1920, his showmanship when he turned to costume during the twenties. His athleticism is a constant of his career, for although during the first year the studio publicity insisted on the acrobatics for their own sake, it was subsequently an original technique for describing and stressing the other two. If this is understood, we can best appreciate the character by breaking it down into these three elements.

A. THE POPULAR PHILOSOPHER (1917-1920)

The Douglas Fairbanks Film Corporation started off with a skit on the New Jersey sabotage explosions, IN AGAIN, OUT AGAIN. It was released at the end of April, 1917, and made bold fun of pacifists (the opening shot was of a peace meeting presided over by a framed portrait of William Jennings Bryan), but not too bold or ridiculous for a nation just gone passionately to war. The Fairbanks part, true to the ripening symbol of him as an average young American of stirring sanity and dash, was perfectly tailored to the national mood. The pacifists were drawn as graybeards of almost inhuman effeminacy, so that the arrival in their midst of "Doug" did not seem to the audience especially bounding or belligerent. It seemed like the tonic action of a normal young man.

Fairbanks the popular philosopher, 1919-21

17

The satirical touch of most of the Fairbanks movies of this period would have been limp or outlandish, and therefore negligible, were it not for the sure touch of normality on an even keel. A great many movies that brandish the charm of emotional normality in solving fictional neuroses are often tasteless and occasionally ludicrous because the implied view of normality is itself a highly neurotic symptom. If Fairbanks had any neuroses, they were, then, the chronic ones of the average man who will never become pathological. The word "normal" can truly be used of Fairbanks in this sense as well as in the literal sense of being, like a man with "normal" vision, the one man in a million who registers the exact norm from which most of us vary more or less. He was the abnormal norm of the man in the street and his growing audience never mistook him for a Don Juan, a character actor, or a comedian or acrobat simply. He was a muscular itinerant preacher sailing gaily into the social novelties and the occupational neuroses of a new era dizzy with growing pains. He could do this without any doubt of his popularity because Fairbanks had the feel of the popular pulse—he knew to a degree the median limits of romance, prejudice, social conservatism; he knew them instinctively because they were his own. It is a good proof that a really popular screen character must have the basic elements in his original character.

His professional confidence strengthened by successful producing, Fairbanks had a hand more and more directly in his stories, scenarios and production. Four of the five pictures he made in 1917 (which more than any of the Triangle ones brought him to the front rank of stardom) were written and directed by Loos and Emerson, with Fairbanks sharing the writing of DOWN TO EARTH. He also wrote the story of THE MAN FROM PAINTED POST. It is therefore safer to generalize about his own view of the character of "Doug."

After MANHATTAN MADNESS, the virility of "Doug," leading to his contempt for the breadwinner's routine, was an axiom. It may be asked how this demonstrates tact in an actor trying to identify himself with his audience.

But most breadwinners have a lurking contempt for breadwinning itself, although to express yourself on this point is usually unpolitic. The movie public could nevertheless admire a man who did express himself because it showed his independence. And the applause was warmly given to the movies that offered a fantasy relief from the painfully familiar situation of a city clerk who "frets along within the confines of the crowded city in anticipation of the day when he will sit astride a bucking broncho and shoot Indians in the wild and woolly West."[5] In WILD AND WOOLLY he is chained to a railroad office desk, and is "nuts on the West." In REACHING FOR THE MOON, he is Alexis Caesar Napoleon Brown, an employee at Bingham's Button Counter, who nourishes his immortal soul on the busts of his given names. In A MODERN MUSKETEER, he is Ned Thacker of Kansas, unbearably fired by the spirit of D'Artagnan. In HIS MAJESTY THE AMERICAN he is William Brooks, "an excitement-hunting thrill hound" soured with the propriety of Manhattan life. HE COMES UP SMILING made the point even more firmly, opening on a title, "Liberty is a Blessed Thing. . . . Think of the bird" which faded into Fairbanks, a bank teller operating behind bars who "in spite of his cage comes up smiling."

It is possible that to an Oriental or a Frenchman, these frolicsome satires would have been acceptable with the mere statement of irony. But irony is to most people a disturbing mood, and an American especially will appreciate it only if it shows how badly something is being done. He expects you to be ironic to a purpose, so as to help diagnose somebody as a phony or to change the Administration. Fairbanks had the normal pragmatic drives at abnormal strength, and he knew all this, not as a critic knows it by deducing good generalizations from the known facts, but as an artist knows it by warning instinct. If the metropolitan East is effete, Fairbanks would not be Fairbanks, and would certainly not be an American, to let it go at that. He must offer an antidote, a goal for the fretting city worker to aim at. Fairbanks

[5] Description of the plot of WILD AND WOOLLY in the original Rialto Theatre program.

18

did not have to invent it. It was present in his own excited belief. It was "the West," in quotes—a state of mind as well as a geographical area. I doubt if his early satires on this city-worker theme could have been so swift or so unlabored if Fairbanks had not truly believed, for a good many of his early years, in "the West." So he had for a time a perfect formula for comedy romance, for throwing off little satires which turned under the impact of the West into energetic sermons (especially WILD AND WOOLLY, THE KNICKERBOCKER BUCKAROO and THE MOLLYCODDLE). In a great many of these American comedies, the West is conceived as a source of natural virtue. And it is a fact that in his first few years he was devoted to it as to a new faith. Later in life he held new ideals with equal enthusiasm, though he always kept enough humor to be able to offer as a regular entertainment a warm defense or a contemptuous smearing of any place mentioned, always including California. The West was, however, a very effective background because it was the best one to demonstrate how he felt about the enervating effects of modern plumbing. Fairbanks was in his violent way a good deal of a reformer, and he was probably more interested than he ever knew in the religious phenomenon of conversion (which to be enjoyed does not have to be felt in its

THE MOLLYCODDLE, 1920

religious manifestations).

In 1917, Fairbanks hastened the approaching merger of "Doug" and Douglas Fairbanks by writing his first inspirational book, called *Laugh and Live.* Between then and the middle twenties he wrote seven more, and their titles[6] are self-explanatory. Whether they were ghost-written or not is irrelevant to the fact that they bear the Fairbanks signature and generalize the screen activities of "Doug" into moral precepts for Everyman's workaday practice. "Doug" was more than a popular entertainer. He had become a necessity in everyday life. And if he

[6] *Making Life Worth-while, Initiative and Self-Reliance, Taking Stock of Ourselves, Whistle and Hoe–Sing as We Go, Assuming Responsibilities, Profiting by Experience, Wedlock in Time.*

The European playboy in THE MOLLYCODDLE, 1920

did not exist in the person of Douglas Fairbanks off-screen, it was necessary to invent him for that role.

Lately, all film actors have had to submit to the publicizing of their private lives as happy coincidences of the parts they play on the screen. The coincidence is less than happy, however, when everybody has it, and there has been a tendency to discredit even the possibility of such charming self-fulfilment. It is fair enough to say from all the evidence that Fairbanks was either the most sincere reproduction we know of a screen character, or he was the most hard-working actor there has ever been in laboring to create that belief. French newspapermen and critics often went to unnecessary lengths to explain that it was "Charlot" they loved, not the dapper little man with the sad private life who was known as Charles Chaplin. Nobody had to make such a distinction in Fairbanks. When he arrived at the Gare du Nord, it was "Doug" they saw and cheered, and just to prove it, Douglas Fairbanks vaulted the platform barrier. When he appeared at the opening nights of his movies in New York, he anticipated the audience's desire to have him carry Mary, his equally adored wife, down the aisle on his shoulder.

To "keep faith" with the "public" is one of the tedious vulgarities of theatre people going out of their way to attract applause, but Fairbanks literally had an obligation in this respect. By 1920 he was a mentor, a model for growing boys, a homespun philosopher of the generation after Will Rogers. Once the virility of the first Western comedies was impressed on the public mind, he looked no further than the bewildered manners of his own day for more pungent lessons. Sure of his public and its trust in the essential health of his reaction to all affectation, he took a series of good-humored swipes at most of the modish post-war fads, light-heartedly parodying a society that now looks to us comfortably like a period, but which to the people who lived it was as anxious and unpredictable as our own. He laughed at hypochondriacs, in Dr. Jollyem's Long Island sanitarium for rich neurotics (DOWN TO EARTH); at "bean-can nobility" in the person of Leander Hick, manu-

D'Artagnan in THE THREE MUSKETEERS, 1921

ideal twentieth century American, a young man who could be romantic in our clothes and successful with our handicaps. There was only one girl in all the world that "Doug," if he could step off-screen, deserved to marry. She was Mary Pickford, "The World's Sweetheart." On the 28th of March, 1920, this "poetic and audacious" event, as a French writer called it, took place.

The marriage was the logical end of the Fairbanks role as popular philosopher. He could do no more. He who had preached in many a short sentence and many a rocketing leap across the screen that rewards can be won in this world, had won the hand of the girl so fragile and winsome that every man wanted her—for his sister. Douglas Fairbanks and Mary Pickford came to mean more than a couple of married film stars. They were a living proof of America's chronic belief in happy endings. As the witty Ferri Pisani said, Fair-

facturer of the One Hump Hat-Pin (AMERICAN ARISTOCRACY); Anglophilia (MR. FIX-IT and THE MOLLYCODDLE); success literature (REACHING FOR THE MOON); bachelor girls, bobbed hair and patronizing social work (THE NUT); the Eastern clubman (KNICKERBOCKER BUCKAROO); quack psychologists (WHEN THE CLOUDS ROLL BY); and by the way, in casual dissolves and pointed subtitles expressed himself unambiguously on the subject of modern dancing, Couéism, ouija boards, night club entertainment, women's clothes and other incidental oddities of the period.

———

In 1917, a peak was named after Fairbanks in Yosemite National Park. In 1920 Roscoe (Fatty) Arbuckle made a hit with a comedy in which he dreamed he too could be "Doug." By the spring of 1920, Fairbanks was the favorite male film star in nation-wide polls in the United States, in France and in England. He was the

Fairbanks with Mary Pickford in the early talkie, THE TAMING OF THE SHREW, 1929

21

Fairbanks is seen here in three successive phases of a beautifully coordinated movement as he practices quoit-throwing

banks was the best propaganda for Christian Science that had come out of America since Mary Baker Eddy. He added: "Ce *bluff*, c'est l'optimisme Yankee; et Pickford-Fairbanks en est le symbole."

B. THE ATHLETE (1916-1932)

Many and varied were the dilemmas of "Doug" over a score or more of his pictures, yet there was a regular technical formula for a Fairbanks triumph. It was the galvanizing of a cheerful young American into a sort of campus whirl-wind who extricates himself in a final scherzo of energy to win romantic and material success. For the audience it is a beautifully deceptive act of flattery, suggesting that all that is needed to clear up the stagnation of city life, a capture by Moroccan bandits, or a Cabinet crisis in a South American republic, is the arrival of an average healthy man. What is nowhere suggested, and available only on painful thought to the holder of an insurance policy savings account, is the fact that aside from his impulses, which were those of a popular evange-

list, "Doug" was a person of superbly responsive physique and of quite extraordinary grace and initiative.

Nowhere was this more evident than at the crises, in his movies, when he appeared to be cornered. One of the special excitements of watching Fairbanks at bay was the fore-knowledge that he was no more earthbound than Superman, his 1940 counterpart. In the most typical films (especially in A MODERN MUSKETEER, BOUND IN MOROCCO, and many times in THE MARK OF ZORRO, THE THREE MUS-KETEERS and ROBIN HOOD) there was a delicious moment when he would fall back before his adversaries, not in retreat but to gain a second in which to reconsider the resources of a room as a machine for escape. Most romantic melo-dramas have these ominous bridge passages and they are usually resolved in a single con-ventional plunge to escape—a decisive revolver shot, a flicking off of the lights, the fortuitous collapse of the villain by an unknown hand. Fairbanks would not have been the incom-parable "Doug" if he had not provided the most characteristic pleasure of his films in just these crises. And "Doug" could not have held the popular imagination so long if he had lacked the extraordinary physical rhythm and grace of Douglas Fairbanks, a remarkable all-round athlete.

It is usual to search earnestly for superior acting ability or human qualities in "Doug," the light comedian, to provide an assurance that he was more than "a mere acrobat." In this method of apology, there is a strong statement of ignorance as well as a hint of sour grapes. To talk about acrobats in this way implies that their skill is something tricky and trivial which any healthy body could acquire overnight. It is comforting to recall Hazlitt who, after a life-time's appreciation of actors and acting, was moved to tears only once, by the exquisite and, as it seemed to him, philosophical skill of a juggler.

Fairbanks took up gymnastics in New York. It is pretty obvious from his movies that he became a first-rate all-round gymnast with a preferential talent for horizontal bar and pommel-horse. By the time he went out West he was also a superior swimmer and horseman. He managed to win over the moderately sullen crew of the Triangle studio by his apparent willingness to take serious physical risks,[7] a sign of comradeship very rare in the actors they had been used to, who more usually resented location shooting because there was no hotel. By the same willingness, he was also occasionally a nuisance—holding up shooting once for a night and day while he wandered off to learn trapping from a forester. He made the maximum use of every outdoors specialist he came across, astounding the Frontier Day stars of the Cheyenne, Wyoming, rodeo by his courage and aptitude for roping and broncho riding. He practised some sport every day for nearly twenty years and practised most whenever he could get professional coaching. Unsatisfied with the respectful boxing and wrestling practice he was getting in Hollywood, he sent East for Bull Montana, who trained in a New York gymnasium where Fairbanks had known him as a fighting equal unmoved by the dignity of actors. His studio soon became an athlete's mecca. World champions came there to pose first and teach afterwards. College track and

[7] These his fellow players often had to share. After one episode, Fairbanks pensioned for life a Sioux Indian who had developed a permanent limp.

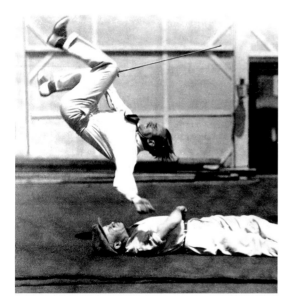 

Fairbanks rehearsing (left) the singlehanded handspring for (right) THE THREE MUSKETEERS, 1921

23

swimming teams went home in a daze after being photographed with the movie hero who, in 1922, had paced Bob Simpson, then world's champion low hurdler, and had given a good account of himself in an all-round competition with Brutus Hamilton, the American decathlon champion.

He made friends with the aeronaut in THE LAMB in order to learn to fly a biplane. For THE MYSTERY OF THE LEAPING FISH he annexed the "professor" and learned what he could of underwater tricks. For THE THREE MUSKETEERS he was faced with the prospect of having to play reasonably well a man known to literature as "the greatest swordsman in France." His fencing had always been, if anything, better than his horsemanship, which was better than first-rate. In THE THREE MUSKETEERS, according to a former French foils champion, he moved easily into the championship class. In training for the same movie, he put up an unofficial challenge to the amateur record for standing high and broad jumps. For THE GAUCHO he learned to throw the bola and the pictures reproduced here, of a casual practice period, show the easy rhythm of perfect relaxation, the mark of a natural athlete.

He could amuse himself and his friends by doing what are called "feats of strength" and there is a snapshot or two of him weight-lifting. But he was watchful of this sort of training, which was then being healthily superseded in most European and American gymnasiums by the free-standing exercises of the Swedes. For above all, he was a great gymnast. He was trained not to show off biceps but to develop his body to a virtuoso pitch of responsiveness. Even professional gymnasts need apparatus and are clannishly leary of uncertified ropes and fences and invitations to perform without well-resined hands. Fairbanks' glory, the mystery of his visual fascination, is that he could throw all the textbook tricks on the makeshift apparatus of ordinary life. He appears to the moviegoer to be a sort of Ariel, leaping where he has a mind without any of the natural checks of gravity. But there is not a leap, a turn or a change of terrain which cannot be precisely named in the gymnastic jargon. It is

simply that these things are normally done on a horizontal bar, or on parallels, or on a trapeze. To Fairbanks the limb of a tree suggests a hocks-off; a narrow lane with high walls is a risky, but workable, set of parallel bars; a spear is a pole to vault with. During the filming of ROBIN HOOD he used the tent-poles to practise both pole-vaulting and, after the application of a little vaseline, climbing the greasy pole.

This spontaneous identification of shape with function seems to be a faculty of comedy in more fields than the gymnastics of Douglas Fairbanks. It is essentially the same gift, and engenders the same pleasure of surprise, as when Chaplin—newly employed in a pawnshop—is handed a watch and instantly uses a can-opener on it with exquisite skill; or when, hungry, he sees an old shoe and miraculously the shape of the sole is a fish and the arc of nails in the plan of bone strategy that the best-mannered fish-eaters know all about. Fairbanks, too, produces the effect, when let loose on a landscape or cornered in a room, of revamping the stubborn natural fixtures of the world we live in to match the highly specialized needs of his dilemma. It looks like reckless gaiety, and one critic has dully said the secret of Fairbanks is that he knew how to assert himself. But to assert yourself in any art with a mite of distinction, it is necessary to have something to assert. A hundred comedians since the movies started have groaned and grinned and asserted themselves to the limit of their glandular command. Their unflagging mediocrity, and Fairbanks' unique grace and zest, are still unexplained. Fairbanks was able to give the appearance of casual self-assertion for much the same reason that Weissmuller can smile and crawl at the same time, or DiMaggio can lope to the diamond.

It is the confidence that flows freely, without emotional pump-priming, from a knowledge of absolutely perfect coordination of will and muscle. Fairbanks used a double (for the run up the drawbridge-chain in ROBIN HOOD) only once throughout his movie career. But a double is irrelevant to Fairbanks' great gymnastic gift. For he is not doing set-tricks. His movies were terrifying to gymnasts because so many of his stunts are improvisations during shooting, without the benefit of prepared holds on ledges, disguised steps or other aids to health. The only time he misses—his running jump from his whip on to the wall in DON Q, SON OF ZORRO—the steadying stumble is slight but so untypical that we are forced, by contrast, to marvel at the visual certainty of poise in a gymnast who can always use Nature's poor gymnasium and land clean, with his weight even, his body free to move the way it wants.

This is why Fairbanks held the senses as Eddie Polo, the favorite "athletic actor" of his day, could not. Fairbanks was, even under stress, an athlete without strain, and in his most daring leap there is the assurance of reserves. But mainly it is that virtuoso use of the landscape as a natural gymnasium whose equipment is invisible to the ordinary man, the use of his own body as a crazy but disciplined bow on something that turns into a handy fiddle, that made him an enchanting image, whatever the plot was saying—and when the story was saying something about a girl in danger, or the need for courage, offered a technique unknown to actors to enforce its romantic spell.

C. THE SHOWMAN 1912-1929

The philosopher, the athlete, the showman overlap. The showman does not stand out in strong relief until the costume films of the 1920s, and the character of "Doug" was finished before Fairbanks turned to costume. These later films added nothing to that screen character which, as we have seen, had been made possible by a certain original temperament, by a social need in the American movie public and by the happy accident of industrial immaturity in the movies which denied it the routine of casting systems and rapid "typing."

A decade later it would have been essential to give the character of "Doug" more pretentious commercial promotion. Luckily, at the time it grew this was not needed. But in the 1920s Fairbanks, now a very wealthy producer, took over on his own artistic responsi-

DON Q, SON OF ZORRO, with Warner Oland and Mary Astor, 1925

bility the further fate and fame of his own screen character.

One generation remembers Fairbanks as the young, dark, clean-shaven "Doug". Another was just beginning to know him in the guise that—at its first public appearance—faintly shocked the movie reporter of the *New York Times*: "It was a slightly heavier Fairbanks, with a business man's moustache, who took the stage to express his thanks." This was after the opening of THE THREE MUSKETEERS. The younger "Doug," kidding the bustling *mores* of the World War days, writing popular sermons for American youth, never reappeared. His last appearance was in THE NUT, Fairbanks' thirty-first film. Douglas Fairbanks made only twelve more films, two for other producers, but three or four of them were the movies of his prime. The change from comedian-satirist to swashbuckling costume-hero may be explained by two developments, one a social situation, the other a stage of the industry's growth.

By 1921 the post-war world was launched. The fillip of victory to the peoples of the conquering Allies was already spent and fizzling uncertainly in the clouds of reparations, European famine, the vanishing rainbow of the League of Nations. There was world-wide social disappointment in the fruits of war, and the time was ripe for literature and entertainment that denied the complexity of a post-war

Fairbanks' first costume picture, THE MARK OF ZORRO, 1920

world. It was a good time to clutch to the bosom the institutions that had always been taken for granted in the theatre world—Italian opera, Gilbert and Sullivan, Grand Guignol. Others, who did not share these threatened heritages, went after their own entertainment of escape. *The Sheik* was a world-wide best-seller, penetrating even to the Near East, where its wilfully romantic tone made it an "escape" book even, perhaps, for the sheiks. Elinor Glyn isolated sex and named it "It," thus implying that this was a separate and more intense pleasure, to be taken neat without any of the normal embarrassments of the old compound "love."

To people tired of the real history they saw around them there was this alternative escape; forward, by the bold, into sensation to be treated as if it had no past and no emotional laws; backward, by the more timid or tra-ditional, into a distant world which could be imagined as untroubled by realism—a world which, to be recaptured, must be conceived as the golden age of its most characteristic institu-tions, such as for example the institution of kingship. In 1921 all over Europe thrones were toppling. Decent sentimentalists—Douglas Fairbanks, say—were touched by the collapse of these symbols. Fairbanks was neither young nor neurotic enough to take the first escape. His costume pictures were a lush adventure into the second.

This, roughly, with much left out, was the chronic social situation.

The business situation was more concrete, and also more acute; it was, in the movies, the

26

fight for the control of distribution. As a rank-ing star, Fairbanks was one of many whose distribution was an immense undertaking for any ordinary producing company. The forma-tion of the United Artists Company as a major distributing organization brought together D. W. Griffith, Charles Chaplin, Mary Pickford and Douglas Fairbanks, stars who were "too expensive for any single company to maintain on a permanent payroll."[8] With the distribu-tion of his films assured and with the probably preconscious urge to romantic nostalgia on a grand scale, Fairbanks started to make costume films. THE MARK OF ZORRO was hardly one, but it was a sign of the times. It was modestly pro-duced; a retrospective lesson from the difficult

[8] Jacobs, Lewis, *The Rise of the American Film*, New York, Harcourt, Brace, 1939.

1850s of California, when oppression was routed and the poor made whole by a daring noble-man in a mask. THE MARK OF ZORRO was an im-mense success, and when Fairbanks looked back to find other historical shells to clothe the spirit of "Doug," there was D'Artagnan. Later there was Robin Hood, the thief of Bag-dad, the son of Zorro, the Black Pirate. All but one were high-born saviors of the people. A fascist or royalist government could probably do much mischief with this continuing theme, which was certainly offered in good faith by Fairbanks as a touching formula of magic, an act of grace from on high, which the post-war world badly needed. Young "Doug," the cracker-barrel gymnast, was now a fly-by-night missionary in fancy dress.

After the success of THE THREE MUSKETEERS

This set for ROBIN HOOD—the largest in American film history—astonished the California skies in 1922

THE THIEF OF BAGDAD, 1924

motion with a rather more theatrical swagger, Fairbanks' stage training never counted much until the period of the costume films, when he relied too often on an acting style that a younger "Doug" had once lightly tossed out of the movies. But the stress was increasingly on Fairbanks the producer.

He was an extremely shrewd business man, and there was nothing naive about the grandiosity of his production ambitions. Allene Talmey has very effectively disposed of the pleasant fallacy that Fairbanks was a cheerful athlete with no head for money.[9] And Frank

[9] *Doug and Mary, and Some Others*, New York, Macy-Masius, 1927.

it seemed clear that costume fantasy was what people wanted most, at least from Douglas Fairbanks. This encouragement was very gratifying to a Fairbanks who had become a remarkable impresario. His studio was still a place to rollic in, but armies of workmen moved there, huge sets were built (ROBIN HOOD, THE THIEF OF BAGDAD). By an act of bravado worthy of "Doug," Fairbanks had made a gesture to solve Hollywood's chronic unemployment problem of 1921-22 and given orders for the largest interior ever to be built in the history of the movies, the biggest cast (ROBIN HOOD). Soon through these halls went Leloir, the French costume expert; Carl Oscar Berg, the Swedish artist; Dwight Franklin, the authority on buccaneer life; Robert Nichols, the poet. Soon there were conferences of engineers, painters, chemists, men stringing a hundred and twenty piano wires to suspend the swimmers of THE BLACK PIRATE from a crane. There was always throughout the twenties a small army of technical experts on the various periods relived in the Fairbanks fantasies; construction crews, painters, odd craftsmen were brought from every corner of Europe.

During this period, Fairbanks himself was primarily a pioneer producer, absorbed in methods of producing costume film, crowd pictures, color film. The character of "Doug" was stripped down to the romantic essentials. Dressed in a cloak and a rapier and set in

THE THIEF OF BAGDAD, 1923–4

28

Case notes that "Douglas could break up a meeting of directors . . . by disappearing up a fire escape . . . but when the final decision was to be made it would be his voice and his opinion that decided the verdict."

The peak of his popularity was, most likely, the presentation of ROBIN HOOD (1922). After the première in New York, a second première had to be given after midnight for the unaccommodated mob. But even in ROBIN HOOD the naked line and rhythm of Fairbanks is occasionally shaggy with parades and scenery. He was to play one more extravaganza. THE THIEF OF BAGDAD, made at prodigious cost to better the example of the German historical costume film (PASSION, ALL FOR A WOMAN, GYPSY BLOOD), suffocated the old beloved sprite in a mess of

décor. It was the last conflict of the showman-producer with the Fairbanks screen character, although several times later the more theatrical convention of acting which he had restored to his costume character froze the gaiety of "Doug" into stage cameos. After THE THIEF, however, he went back to a simpler presentation of the character. Paul Rotha excellently noted that "curiously enough it is in this wish to encourage the 'art' of the cinema that Fairbanks strikes the wrong note. His most recent films have not had the rough power, the intensity or the vigor" of his early films. Louis Delluc, familiar only with the costume Fairbanks, had never seen the early films; discovering them accidentally he hailed them as "something not of the theatre, something which is

Fairbanks with Wallace Beery in ROBIN HOOD, 1922

THE BLACK PIRATE, 1926

simple, direct, sincere, with a vital rhythm . . .
in fact a true moving picture."

In spite of the vigor and humor of his last
films, of THE IRON MASK, and THE TAMING OF
THE SHREW, the pretension of the great impresario throws an artificial shadow over the
swinging stride, the cat-like grace of the simple
"knickerbockerbuckaroo" who once had no high-
er ambition than to get his girl. And in his last
film, made in England for Korda, there is
hardly a clue to the undoubted fact that Fairbanks is a truer artist than any of the more
pretentious ones who surrounded him. For the
first six years of his movie career he was a
fumbling boyish poet acting from a sincere
personal impulse. The showman of the last
eight or nine years (1922-1930) tended to per-
suade him to act out of a praiseworthy awe for

the social-cultural values. There can hardly be
a question which of the two is better Fairbanks
or better art. The trajectory of WHEN THE
CLOUDS ROLL BY, A MODERN MUSKETEER, or
THE MARK OF ZORRO is the breathless quixotic
line of a gymnast who was also an evangelist;
that of THE THIEF OF BAGDAD is a boy gro-
tesquely buried in a library of costume.

"Doug" could breathe freely on the tops of
church steeples, hanging from a mountain crag,
or diving through a window pane; the only
things that choke him are the scent and
epigram of the boudoir.

Douglas Fairbanks suffers from the advan-
tage, until now, of being written about very
little. The literary discovery of the movies,
late though it was, found its darling in Charles
Chaplin. It was unlikely that esthetes, so

30

gingerly sorting out the odd and curious in this raffish art, should retrace their steps to find, so close to Chaplin's back door, another pet. Indeed the most revealing and reliable references to Fairbanks can be found, not in critical books on the movies (with the exception of one essay of Delluc and a couple of pages of Rotha's history) but in the index of producers' memoirs and in histories like Terry Ramsaye's and Hampton's of the movies as a growing industry.

This surely does not amount to neglect of Fairbanks. He will bear intellectual scrutiny as well as any other artist with a talent of his own, but not the loaded curiosity of those who look at movies with their own constructed hierarchy of movie values. He does not have to be rescued, as Chaplin had, from any cult admiration. When he was most famous, the only fervid cult of him was the universal brotherhood of small boys who translated the effect Fairbanks had on his audience into the direct flattery of leaping over fire hydrants and joining a gymnasium.

Through the 1910s and early twenties, the movies were fighting many a scandal and much imprecise suspicion to get themselves accepted as respectable by the middle class of the western world. They bore then a sneaking reputation, something like that of latter-day burlesque. To many an anxious parent at this time, "Doug" stood for the film industry's total respectability. He was not merely inoffensive, which is what the parents were looking for: he was a positive ideal worthy of any small fry's devoted emulation. To the people in the business, notably Joe Schenck, it occurred rather late that "this fellow knows more about making pictures than all the rest of us put together." To nobody at all did it occur that Fairbanks had solved as early as anybody in the game the problem—which, when the literati have had their say, is the unblinkable problem of a popular art—of mating audience and actor, as truly as a promoter of bear-baiting or baseball, so that a movie seems to be, not a cultural knick-knack handed down from above, but an actual creation of the audience, a copy of their liveliest impulses. This may be, of course, what Mr. Schenck had in mind.

CHRONOLOGY

1883 *May 23:* Born Denver, Colo., Douglas Elton Ulman, son of H. Charles Ulman and Ella Adelaide (Marsh).

1888-99: (1) Jarvis Military Academy.
(2) East Denver High School.
(3) Colorado School of Mines.

1900 *Sept. 10:* Richmond, Va. First stage appearance, as Florio in *The Duke's Jester*, at the Academy of Music.

1901
Jan.: Cambridge, Mass. Entered Harvard College.

May: Left Harvard College.

Summer: Took cattle-boat to Europe, bummed through England, France and Belgium. New York City. Became order clerk with De Coppet and Doremus. Became clerk in hardware store.

1902
Mar. 3: New York City. First Broadway appearance, as Glen Masters (in support of Effie Shannon and Herbert Kelcey) in *Her Lord and Master.*

Sept.: Phillippe in *A Rose of Plymouth Town.*

1903: Toured the U. S. in *Mrs. Jack.*

1904 *Feb:* Landry Court in *The Pit*, under management of William A. Brady.

1904-09: Played juveniles on Broadway.

1907 *July 11:* Providence, R. I. Married Anna Beth Sully, daughter of Daniel J. Sully, "the Saviour of the South."

1909 *Dec. 9:* New York City. Douglas Fairbanks, Jr., born.

1909-11: Toured the U. S. as Bud Haines in *A Gentleman From Mississippi.*

1911-12: In vaudeville with act called "A Regular Business Man."

1912-14: Played leads on Broadway.

1914 *Dec.:* Played Jerome Belden in *The Show Shop*, his last Broadway play.

1915
Spring: Signed with Harry Aitken, representing Triangle Corporation. Went to Hollywood.

Sept. 23: THE LAMB, directed by W. Christy Cabanne, supervised by D. W. Griffith with Seena Owen.

Nov. 13: DOUBLE TROUBLE, directed by D. W. Griffith, from a novel by Herbert Quick. Supervised by W. Christy Cabanne.

1916
Feb. 10: HIS PICTURE IN THE PAPERS, directed by John Emerson. Scenario by Anita Loos.

Mar. 13: THE HABIT OF HAPPINESS, with Margery Wilson.

April 13: THE GOOD BAD MAN, with Bessie Love.

May 29: REGGIE MIXES IN, directed by W. Christy Cabanne. Scenario by Roy Somerville. With Bessie Love.

June 29: FLIRTING WITH FATE, directed by W. Christy Cabanne. Story by Robert M. Baker. With Jewel Carmen.

July 10: THE HALF BREED, directed by Allan Dwan. Scenario by Anita Loos. With Alma Rubens and Jewel Carmen.

Aug. ? THE MYSTERY OF THE LEAPING FISH, with Alma Rubens and Bessie Love.

Sept. 11: MANHATTAN MADNESS, directed by Allan Dwan. With Jewel Carmen.

Nov. 6: AMERICAN ARISTOCRACY, directed by Lloyd Ingraham. Scenario by Anita Loos. With Jewel Carmen.

Dec. 4: THE MATRIMANIAC, directed by Paul Powell. Story by Octavus Roy Cohen and J. U. Giesy. With Constance Talmadge.

Dec. 25: THE AMERICANO, directed by John Emerson. Scenario by Anita Loos. Photographed by Victor Fleming. With Alma Rubens.

1917
Apr. 23: IN AGAIN, OUT AGAIN (First production of Douglas Fairbanks Film Corporation). Directed by John Emerson. Scenario by Anita Loos. With Arline Pretty and Bull Montana.

July 5: WILD AND WOOLLY, directed by John Emerson. Scenario by Anita Loos from a story by H. B. Carpenter. With Eileen Percy.

Aug. 16: DOWN TO EARTH, directed by John Emerson. Scenario by Anita Loos from a story by Douglas Fairbanks. With Eileen Percy.

Oct. 1: THE MAN FROM PAINTED POST, directed by Joseph Henabery. Story by Douglas Fairbanks. With Eileen Percy.

Nov. 19: REACHING FOR THE MOON, directed by John Emerson. Scenario by John Emerson and Anita Loos. With Eileen Percy.

1918

Jan. 3: A MODERN MUSKETEER. Story and direction by Allan Dwan. With Zasu Pitts and Marjorie Daw.

Jan. 12: Washington Park, Los Angeles. Douglas Fairbanks Rodeo for American Red Cross.

Mar. 21: HEADIN' SOUTH, directed by Arthur Rosson. Scenario by Allan Dwan. With Katharine MacDonald.

Apr. 22: MR. FIX-IT. Scenario and direction by Allan Dwan. With Wanda Hawley and Marjorie Daw.

June 17: SAY YOUNG FELLOW. Scenario and direction by Joseph Henabery. With Marjorie Daw.

July 29: BOUND IN MOROCCO. Story and direction by Allan Dwan. With Pauline Curley.

Sept. 9: HE COMES UP SMILING, directed by Allan Dwan. Scenario by Frances Marion from a novel by Charles Sherman. With Marjorie Daw.

Nov. 30: White Plains, N. Y. Divorced by Beth Sully.

Dec. 15: ARIZONA, directed by Douglas Fairbanks. Adapted from the play by Augustus Thomas. With Marjorie Daw and Marguerite de la Motte.

1919

May 26: THE KNICKERBOCKER BUCKAROO, directed by Albert Parker. Scenario by Douglas Fairbanks. With Marjorie Daw.

Sept. 28: HIS MAJESTY THE AMERICAN. Story and direction by Joseph Henabery. Photographed by Victor Fleming. With Lillian Langdon and Marjorie Daw. (This and all subsequent films distributed through the newly incorporated United Artists, formed to distribute the productions of the Big Four –Fairbanks, Chaplin, Mary Pickford, and D. W. Griffith.)

Dec. 29: WHEN THE CLOUDS ROLL BY, directed by Victor Fleming. Story by Douglas Fairbanks. With Kathleen Clifford.

1920

Mar. 28: Hollywood, Cal. Married Gladys Smith (Mary Pickford).

June 14: THE MOLLYCODDLE, directed by Victor Fleming. Story and scenario by Douglas Fairbanks. With Wallace Beery, Ruth Renick and Betty Boulton.

Nov. 29: THE MARK OF ZORRO, directed by Fred Niblo. Adapted from The Curse of Capistrano by Johnston McCulley. With Marguerite de la Motte and Noah Beery.

1921

Mar. 19: THE NUT, directed by Ted Reed. Story by Kenneth Davenport. With Marguerite de la Motte and Barbara La Marr.

Aug. 28: THE THREE MUSKETEERS, directed by Fred Niblo. Adapted by Edward Knoblock. Photographed by Arthur Edeson. With Marguerite de la Motte, Barbara La Marr and Adolphe Menjou.

Sept. 24: Sailed with Mary Pickford for Europe.

Dec.: Returned from tour of England, Europe, northern Africa.

1922 *Nov. 5:* ROBIN HOOD, directed by Allan Dwan. Scenario by Douglas Fairbanks. Photographed by Arthur Edeson. With Enid Bennett and Wallace Beery.

1923-4

1924 *Mar. 22:* THE THIEF OF BAGDAD, directed by Raoul Walsh. Settings by William Cameron Menzies. Photographed by Arthur Edeson. With Julianne Johnston, Anna May Wong and Sojin.

1925 *June 21:* DON Q, SON OF ZORRO, directed by Donald Crisp. Based on a novel by K. and Hesketh Prichard. With Mary Astor.

1926 *Mar. 21:* THE BLACK PIRATE (in color), directed by Albert Parker. Story by Douglas Fairbanks (*pseud.* Elton Thomas). Photographed by Henry Sharp. With Billie Dove and Donald Crisp.

1927 *Nov. 27:* THE GAUCHO, directed by F. Richard Jones. Story by Douglas Fairbanks (Elton Thomas). With Lupe Velez, Eve Southern and Mary Pickford.

1929

Mar. 9: THE IRON MASK, directed by Allan Dwan. Story by Douglas Fairbanks (Elton Thomas). Photographed by Henry Sharp. With Marguerite de la Motte and Belle Bennett.

Oct. 26: THE TAMING OF THE SHREW (all talking), directed by Sam Taylor. Settings by William Cameron Menzies. Costumes by Laurence Irving. With Mary Pickford.

1930 *Dec.:* San Francisco. Sailed on world tour with Victor Fleming.

1931

Feb. 21: REACHING FOR THE MOON, directed by Edmund Goulding. Story by Edmund Goulding and Irving Berlin. Photographed by Ben Kline. With Bebe Daniels, Edward Everett Horton, Bing Crosby and June MacCloy.

Dec. 12: AROUND THE WORLD IN 80 MINUTES, directed by Victor Fleming and Douglas Fairbanks. Story by Douglas Fairbanks. Dialogue by Robert E. Sherwood. Photographed by Henry Sharp and Chuck Lewis.

1932

Mar. San Francisco. Sailed for Tahiti.

Aug. 19: MR. ROBINSON CRUSOE directed by Edward Sutherland. Story by Douglas Fairbanks (Elton Thomas). Photographed by Max Dupont. With William Farnum and Maria Alba.

Aug. San Francisco. Sailed for game hunt in Japan, China, Manchuria and Mongolia. Returned through Siberia to Paris.

Dec. 20 New York. Returned from world tour.

1933 *Feb. 4:* New York. Sailed to Europe.

1934 *Nov. 30:* THE PRIVATE LIFE OF DON JUAN (made in England). Produced by London Films. Directed by Alexander Korda. Story by Frederick Lonsdale and Lajos Biro. Photographed by Georges Perinal. With Merle Oberon, Benita Hume, Binnie Barnes, Joan Gardner and Natalie Paley.

1935 *Jan. 10:* Divorced from Mary Pickford.

1936

Mar. 7: Paris, France. Married Lady Ashley.

Mar. 15: In a public statement declared he was "through with acting."

1937 *Jan. 14:* New York. Returned from Europe. (During most of 1933-36, he had lived in England and France, returning to the U. S. for brief business trips.)

1938 *Dec. 7:* London. Announced formation of new producing company, to be known as Fairbanks-International.

1939

Fall: Planning the first production of Fairbanks-International, THE CALIFORNIAN, to star his son, Douglas Fairbanks, Jr.

Dec. 12: Beverly Hills. Died in his sleep.

INDEX

The names of films are in capital letters; those of plays and books in italics.

INDEX

EIGHT THOUSAND COPIES OF THIS BOOK WERE PRINTED FOR THE TRUSTEES OF THE
MUSEUM OF MODERN ART, BY THE PLANTIN PRESS, NEW YORK, NOVEMBER, 1940.